Rhymes While Doing time

Incarcerated Body.

Free Mind.

Mayor Sanchez Waller

ISBN:
9798878033510

DEDICATION

ALL PRAISE IS TO ALLAH. THIS BOOK IS DEDICATED TO EVERYONE WHO BELIEVED, INVESTED AND SUPPORTED ME THROUGHOUT MY LIFE. MY MOTHER. MY FATHER. MY SIBLINGS. MY BEAUTIFUL NIECE. MY HANDSOME NEPHEW. MY FRIENDS AND EXTENDED FAMILY. TO MY LAWYERS AND THEIR FIRMS. TO THE PEOPLE WHO GAVE ME WORDS OF ENCOURAGEMENT DURING MY HARD TIMES. THIS DEDICATION IS FOR THOSE WHO SHOWED ME WHAT LOYALTY AND UNCONDITIONAL LOVE IS.

CONTENT

My mind is free as my body is in jail
My spirit is roaming as I'm imprisoned in a cell
I'm taking deep breaths then I slowly exhale
Once my time is served I know I'll prevail
Who's fault is it that I'm here?
I must man up and take the blame.
Every cause has an effect.
Every scar was once pain.
Behind these 4 walls I'm a product of my choice.
Once these 4 walls are behind me I will gladly rejoice!!!

★ I blame myself for being here. I had too much
pride to speak up, ask for help, & admit to my
lack of understanding. I thought that we
(my Public Defender & I) could do things on our own
with no proper, prior, nor strategic planning. I
was always taught that prior planning prevents
piss poor performance and piss poor performance
promotes pain.

— Mayor

The free prisoner

My mind is free as my body is in jail.
My spirit is roaming as I'm imprisoned in a cell.
I'm taking deep breaths then I slowly exhale.
Once my time is served I know I'll prevail. Whose fault is it that I'm in here?
I must man up and take the blame.
Every cause has an effect.
Every scar was once pain.
Behind these four walls I'm a product of my choice.
Once these four walls are behind me I will gladly rejoice!

What you heard about jail?
Let me guess; bad people and gang fights.
Maybe you heard about the stabbings.
People getting poured out at night.
Do you know about the strips?
Passing the wicks through the door.
Ten dollars on the outside is a million on the store.
One person orders summer sausage.
The other orders chips & soups.
Now the pocket cooking.
When I say Hell Cat I'm not talking about coupes.
The things they don't tell you about jail.
Is how talented the people are.
There are poets & artist
Geniuses who can pass the lawyer bar.
Cooks with many recipes
Prayers that move the Earth.
Men who show some emotions.
Boys who show growth.
It didn't take a correction center;
For me to better myself.
If "x" marks the spot;
The hidden talent is in jail.

— Mayor

.JAIL TALK

What you heard about Jail?
Let me guess; bad people and gang fights.
Maybe you heard about the stabbings.
People getting poured out at night.
Do you know about the strips?
Passing the Wicks through the door.
$10 on the outside is a million on the store.
One person orders summer sausage.
The other orders chips and soups.
Now the pocket cooking.
When I say hellcat; I'm not talking coupes.
The things they don't tell you about jail.
Is how talented the people are.
There are poets and artists.
Geniuses who can pass the lawyer bar.
Cooks with many recipes.
Prayers that move the earth.
Men who show emotion.
Boys who shows growth.
It didn't take a correction center for me to better myself.
If "X" marks the spot; the hidden talent is in jail.

This is the concrete jungle
No clear water or green trees
We have on blue suits & white ID bands
It's a place where they're creating savages out of human born
Writings on the walls from old inmates
Prayer calls for those who have faith
Fights for those who stand their ground
C.O. waking you up just to do their round
Arguments that makes no sense
White socks that pick up lint
Boots on concrete floors
Scavengers lurking to see who made store
1 shower for 50 men
Securus phones tapped in
Must be careful what you say on the phone
And who you call your friend
Toothbrushes turn into shanks
Officers abusing ranks
But no matter how bad things get
WE MUST ALWAYS GIVE THANKS!!!

- Mason

AMAZON

This is the concrete jungle.
No clear water or green trees.
We have on blue suits and white ID bands.
It's a place where they're creating savages out of human beings.
Writings on the walls from old inmates.
Prayer calls for those who have faith.
Fights for those who stand their ground.
C.O.'s waking you up just to do their round.
Arguments that makes no sense.
White socks that pick up lint.
Boats on concrete floors.
Scavengers lurking to see who made store.
One shower for 50 men.
Securus phones tapped in.
Must be careful what you say on the phone.
And who you call your friend.
Toothbrushes turns into Shanks.
Officers abusing ranks.
But no matter how bad things get;
We must always give thanks!!!

I'm not afraid to go to prison
But I'm terrified to go to sleep
Everytime I close my eyes
I dream of the person I should be
Out in the free world I made something of myself
I had little to spare but gave lots to everyone else
I have a family that loves me
Many friends that wished for my success
A few enemies that went against me
But I ALWAYS gave my best
Money was never my motive
I just loved to see people smile
Some only deserved an inch
But I gave them many miles
My dreams are now nightmares
My future hunts me in my sleep
My present is very gloomy
My past is hunting me...

- Mayor

Sweet nightmares

I'm not afraid to go to prison.
But I'm terrified to go to sleep.
Every time I close my eyes.
I dream of the person I should be.
Out in the free world I made something of myself.
I had little to spare but I gave lots to everyone else.
I have a family that loves me.
Many friends that wished for my success.
A few enemies that went against me.
But I always gave my best.
Money was never my motive.
I just love to see people smile.
Some only deserved an inch.
But I gave them many miles.
My dreams are now nightmares.
My future hunts me in my sleep.
my presence is very gloomy.
My past is hunting me..

Do you really believe in God?
Is what I ask my pod.
Will you practice what you preach?
Or is it a faiscade?
I witness people praying then purposely commit a sin.
It truly confuses me...
Why start something and not end?
Start within and find who you are.
Danger signals may say you're going too far.
There are many different paths on the road ahead.
Many speed bumps but you must still practice what you said.
There will be times when you approach a fork.
Steer left or go straight; make the right choice.
You can't look back in the review too long.
What's behind you is gone.
Practice what you preach.
YOUR DESTINATION YOU WILL REACH!!!

- Mayer

KNeed answers

I did something different this morning.
I prayed on my knees.
I open my mouth, spoke from my heart, and said a prayer for
those in need.
I never seen myself in this situation.
An emotional roller-coaster of life.
When the ride takes me down.
I'll buckle up with my head high.
I can't believe I'm condemned to a penitentiary.
They say don't question God.
but God why me?
They say God makes no mistakes.
At times I wondered did he mistaken me.

Phone calls to lawyers, family members, and public defenders.

Surrounded by life sentencers, felons, and first offenders.

When the T.V. comes on we tune in for sports, movies, and shows.

Then a food commercial comes on & we imagine our trays not being cold.

Young heads on hot shit as the elders give advice.

The old heads see a younger them & try to save a life

We play spades on metal tables talking shit to the other team.

Listening to life stories, imaginations, and dreams.

Despite our differences we come together as people, men, and brothers.

This is the life of a Fulton County inmate; we are here to build eachother..

- Mayor

The county

Phone calls to lawyers, family members, and public
defenders.
Surrounded by lifers, felons, and 1st offenders.
When the TV comes on we Tune in for sports, movies, and
shows.
Then a food commercial comes on and we imagine our trays
not being cold.
Young heads on hot shit so the elders gives advice.
The old heads see a younger them and they try to save a life.
We play spades on metal tables talking shit to the other team.
Listening to life stories, imagination, and the dreams.
Despite our differences we come together as people, men,
and brothers.
This is the life of a Fulton County inmate;
we are here to build each other.

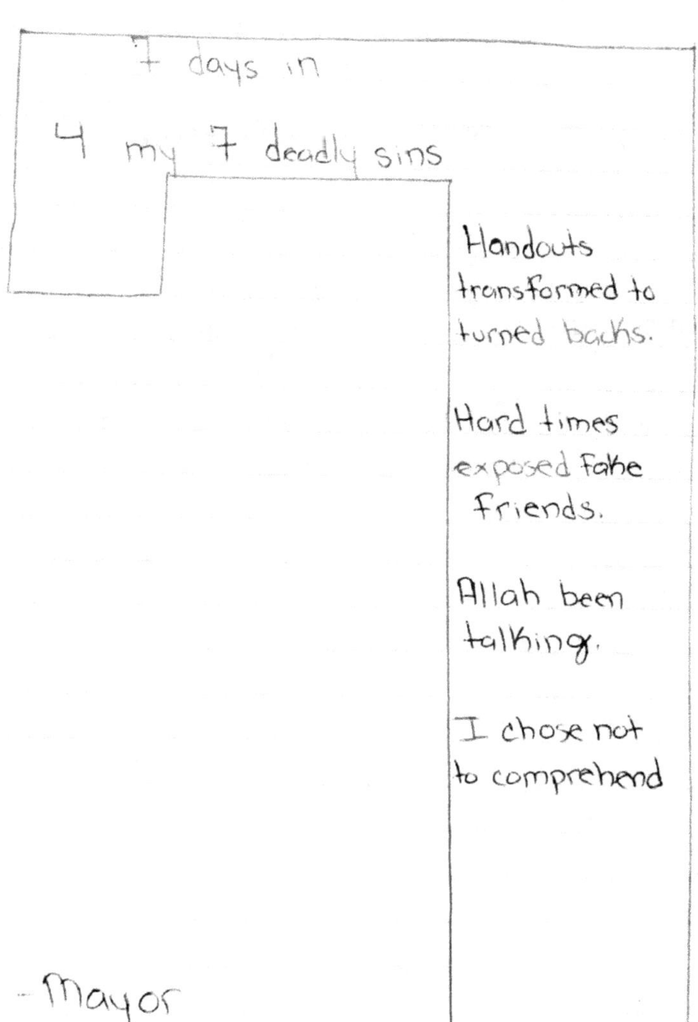

- Mayor

Seven deadly sins

Seven days in.
For my 7 deadly sins.
Handouts transformed to turned backs. Hard times exposed
fake friends.
Allah been talking to me.
I just chose not to comprehend.

Being alive you feel numb.

The dead cant feel any pain.

There's a HUGE difference being caught in the storm,

And actually feeling the rain.

Gratefullness is flowing thru my heart.

Blood is pumping in my veins.

God blessings are coming down.

It's his gift for the ordaine.

~~love~~

Love is the master key.

It puts a smile on a face.

You can't hit life rushing in.

You must have patience & faith.

☆ Mom Dukes asked me to write about
patience & faith.

~Mayor

Keep faith alive

Being alive you feel numb.
The dead can't feel any pain.
There's a huge difference being caught in the storm;
And actually feeling the rain.
Gratefulness is flowing through my heart.
Blood is pumping in my veins.
God's blessings are coming down.
It's his gift for the ordained.
Love is the master key.
It can put a smile on a face.
You can't hit life rushing in.
You must have patience and faith…

Prepare for the worst...

Always pray for the best ..

Trials and tribulations...

Is only a test....

- Mayor

Prior preparation

Prepare for the worst…
Always pray for the best…
Trials and tribulations…
It's only a test…

I have a story to tell
I was blessed to have a pen
My thoughts was all over the place
Ray Ray gave me a book to write in
In the back he wrote motivation
He wrote his number for us to stay in contact
Ray Ray gave me hope
He kept my spirits attained
"Don't Quit" is our motto
We live off BIG FAITH & BIG HOPE
Sometimes we have rough days
Other days we laugh at life's jokes
You're a man who rides for the fam
The 4 Horsemen are lucky to have you
Remember your kids and the world is watching
So more smart and watch what you do
BIG PLAY RAY I'm glad we met
You're my brother and my friend
Our bond is just getting started
OUR BOND SHALL NEVER END!!!

　　　　　　　- Mayor

＊ Ray this is dedicated to you. You've been a blessing
to me. Remember a caged bird can still sing...

Say Ray

I have a story to tell.
I was blessed to have a pen.
My thoughts were all over the place.
Ray Ray gave me a book to write in.
Inside the book he wrote motivation.
He wrote his number for us to stay in contact.
Ray Ray gave me hope.
He kept my spirit attached.
"Don't Quit" is our motto.
We live off of big faith and big hope.
Sometimes we have rough days.
Other days we laugh at life joke.
You're a man who rides for the fam.
The Four Horsemen are lucky to have you.
Remember your kids and the world is watching.
So move smart and watch what you do.
Big Play Ray I'm glad we met.
You're my brother and my friend.
Our bond is just getting started.
Our bond will never end!

Everyone says keep going,
Giving scriptures and words to encourage you.
They say keep your head up.
It's easy to say when you're not in my shoes.
I'm drowned like a fish out of water.
I'm trapped like a bird in a cage.
I'm collapsing like a mountain's avalanche.
My happiness is now rage!

Meyer

New habitat

Everyone says keep going.
Giving quotes and words to encourage you.
They say keep your head up.
It's easy to say when you're not in my shoes.
I'm drained like a fish out of water.
I'm trapped like a bird inside a cage.
I'm collapsing like a mountain's avalanche.
My happiness is now range exclamation

Goodbye to the old me, the person who once cared.

At first I was afraid to lose it all but I'm not scared.

I no longer see the good in people nor do I smile at
the sky.

Goodbye to the old me that caring father had to die.

-Mayar

Self sacrifice

Goodbye to the old me, the person who once cared.
At first I was afraid to lose it all but now I'm not scared.
I no longer see the good in people nor do I smile at the sky.
Goodbye to the old me that loving Fucker had to die.

Pops said don't lose yourself
He said dark times will come
He ensured me I was built to last
When God calls me I can't run
Pops said God has a purpose
Even tho I can't see
I know I was made out of pops sperm
But BIG GOD created me
His son died for my sin
His blood runs thru my insides
I am the son of Tommy, Mommy, and God
I shall shine and will not hide"
-Mayer

+ Dedicated to [illegible]

God's plan

Pops said don't lose yourself.
He said dark times will come.
he assured me I was built to last.
when Allah calls me I can't run.
Pop said God has a purpose.
Even though I can't see.
I know I was made from pop sperm.
But BIG GOD created me.
He shows me mercy for my sins.
There's an unexplained feeling running through my insides.
I am the son of Tammy and Wesley; Who was created by God.
I shall shine and I will not hide!

Do you really believe in God?
Is what I ask my god.
Will you practice what you preach?
Or is it a fasscade?
I witness people praying then purposely commit a sin.
It truly confuses me...
Why start something and not end?
Start within and find who you are.
Danger signals may say you're going too far.
There are many different paths on the road ahead.
Many speed bumps but you must still practice what you said.
There will be times when you approach a fork.
Steer left or go straight, make the right choice.
You can't look back in the river too long.
What's behind you is gone.
Practice what you preach.
YOUR DESTINATION YOU WILL REACH!!!

- Mayer

Moving with no destination

Do you really believe in God?
That's what I asked my pod.
Will you practice what you preach?
Or is it a facade?
I've witnessed people praying then purposely commit a sin.
It truly confuses me…
Why start something and not end?
Start within and find who you are.
Danger signals may say you're going too far.
There are many different paths on the road ahead.
Many speed bumps but you must still practice what you said.
There will be times when you approach a fork.
Steer left or go straight; Make the right choice.
Don't look back in the rear view too long. What's behind you
is gone.
Practice what you preach.
Your destination you will reach!

Today I moved to a new pod
In 300 on the 6th floor
I went up 4 levels
As I entered the elevator door
Them boats I wrote about
I'm now staying on one
Atleast I get more Freedom
What must be done has to be done
Shipping to Jackson can happen whenever
You must prepare yourself for the day
It won't be no more than 2 weeks
Then you'll be shipped away
Is this the life for me?
That I'll never Know
They say God plans everything
I'm just a puppet in his show

                    - Mayor

General population

Today I moved to a new pod.
300 on the 6th floor.
I went up 4 levels.
As I entered the elevator door.
The boats I wrote about.
I'm now sleeping on one.
At least I get more freedom.
What must be done has to be done. Shipping to Jackson can
happen whenever. I must prepare myself for that day.
It won't be more than a few weeks.
Then I shall be shipped away.
Is this the life for me?
That I'll never know.
They say God plans everything.
I'm just a puppet in his show.

I don't know where to start
These 24 hours has been rough
Rough times seem to keep coming
Good times don't come enough
I reminisce on great times
Moments with family & friends
As I think about those times
I wish they never end
Joaning on each other
Fat spliffs in the air
Taking shots with my brother
Giving my girl the fuck me stare
Where does time go?
Some will never know...

- Mayor

Time

I don't know where to start.
These 24 hours has been rough.
Tough times seems to keep coming.
Good times don't come enough.
I reminisce on great times.
Moments with family and friends.
As I think about those times.
I wish they'd never end.
Joaning on each other.
Fat spliffs in the air.
Taking shots with the bros.
Giving my girl the fuck me stare.
Where does time go?
Some will never know…

I'm living the life of the first 48

They're looking for my actions on surveillance tape

Questioning people about my location

A small misunderstanding made a B.I.G. situation.

Now I'm living in general population.

Serving time over a false allegation.

—Mayer

Victimized

I'm living the life of the first 48.
They're looking for my actions on surveillance tape.
Questioning people about my location.
A small misunderstanding made a big situation.
Now I'm living in general population.
Serving time over a false allegation.

"Shhh... Keep quiet
I heard there's a rat in the zone
    Smiling and telling fake stories
    Prolonging your every house
    You're telling your business
    While you hear are open ears
Whole time you're thinking you're gaining cool points
    Meanwhile you feeding the rat in your face
        Fake alias and fake paperwork
        Nigga really 60 days in
        You fed the rat all your info
    Because you thought you made a friend
You told the rat where the bodies are buried
    Not knowing you're killing yourself
    Even told what kind of tool you used
    Naming "what's his name" as your help
        You finally get your court date
        As you prepare yourself for trial
    Then the rat approaches the bench
    That's why you should NEVER trust a snake

        Majo;

Ratatouille

Shhhh…. Keep quiet.
I heard there's a rat in the zone.
Smiling and telling false stories.
Prolonging your way home.
You're telling your business.
Knowing you have an open case.
The whole time you're thinking you're gaining cool points.
Meanwhile you're feeding the rats in your face.
Fake alias and fake paperwork.
Folks really 60 days in.
"You fed" the rats all of your info.
Because you thought you made a friend. You told the right
where the bodies are buried.
Not knowing you're killing yourself.
Even told what kind of tools you used. Naming "what's his
name" as your help.
You finally get your court date.
As you prepare yourself for trial.
Then the rat approaches the bench.
That's why you should never trust a smile.

What is it being mixed?

I know it hurts not hearing your kid's voice.

When was the last time you felt your girl's kiss?

Or smoking a blunt with your boys?

Damn I miss my parent's house.

Grandma's cooking on Sundays night.

I wouldn't mind riding thru the hood.

Going to the gas station? seeing crackheads fight.

Damn this shit hurts.

This will be my first holiday here.

I know it seems far.

But I feel my time is near.

— Mango

Hood memories

What is it being missed?
I know it hurts not hearing your kids voice.
When was the last time you felt your girl's kiss?
Or smoking a blunt with your boys?
Damn I miss my parents house. Grandma's cooking on
Sundays night. i wouldn't mind riding through the hood.
Going to the gas station and seeing random fight.
Damn this shirt hurts.
This would be my first holiday here.
I know it seems far.
But I feel my time is near.

I'm a product of Campbellton
        Ben Hill Zone 4
Lil Baby would say 7 pockets full
Getcha zaza at the gas store
My lil niggas got big sticks
On dirt bikes hitting tricks
I'll never bring a hoe to the spot
    That's how yo shit get hit
    Pussy can be a setup
Getting laid you let your guard down
    Then the opps creep up on you
Now you're butt naked on the ground
I once heard money is the root to evil
    But it all starts with hate
    The nigga you fed a million times
    Will eat you for what's on your plate.

- Mayor

Triple cross

I'm a product of campbellton.
Ben hill zone 4.
Little baby would say 4 pockets full.
Get your zaza at the gas store.
My little homies got big sticks.
On dirt bikes hidden tricks.
I'll never bring a stranger to the spot. That's how your shit get hit.
Anything can be a setup.
Getting laid you let your guard down. Then the OPS creep up on you.
now you're naked laying on the ground.
I used to hear money is the root to all evil. But it all starts with hate.
The people you fed a million times.
will eat you for what's on your plate.

Born Day Part 1

I would've said this is the worst birthday because of where I'm at but that would be a lie.

I could be dead and my loved ones could be at my gravesite letting out cries

They could be laying next to my tomb & grieving because I'm gone.

Instead we are on the securus app waiting for my arrival date back home.

I could have a lost mind

I could have a lot of time.

I could be in a worst situation.

But I know after this dark night the sun will shine.

Born day part 1

I would have said this is the worst birthday because of where
I'm at but that would be a lie.
I could be dead and my loved ones could be at my grave site
letting out cries.
They could be laying next to my tomb and grieving because
I'm gone.
Instead we are on the securus app waiting for my arrival date
back home.
I could have a lost mind.
I could have a lot of time.
I could be in a worst situation.
But I know after this dark night the sun will shine.

Born Day Part 2

I've always spent my birthday with my loved ones, smoking and eating good.

I'd get fresh with a new expensive outfit then pull up to my folks in the hood.

We would hit the most expensive clubs getting fucked up in the VIP.

Then we would grab a few good looking women, hit the telly, and get nasty.

It's my 29th year of living and I'm in jail as an inmate.

No new fit, fine women, no blunts, just another date.

If I had a cake where I can close my eyes and make a wish.

I'd wish to be free surrounded by family and enjoying a big dish.

Born day part 2

I've always spent my birthday with my loved ones; Smoking and eating good.
I'd get fresh with a new expensive outfit then pull up to my folks in the hood.
We would hit the most expensive clubs getting wasted in the VIP.
Then we would grab a few good looking women, hit the telly, and get nasty.
It's my 29th year of living and I'm in jail as an inmate.
No new fits, fine women, no blunts, just another date.
If I had a cake where I can close my eyes and make a wish.
I'd wish to be free surrounded by my family and enjoying a big dish.

They allowed one person to fuck up EVERYTHING
I worked for my entire life.

I came from the trenches, fought my way up,
and made a big sacrifice.

I gave up my old habbits such as robbing
and stealing.

The sacrifice moved my spirit and gave
me a great healing.

— Mayor

Give to receive

They allowed one person to mess up everything I worked for
my entire life.
I came from the trenches, fought my way up, and made a big
sacrifice.
I gave up my old habits such as robbing and stealing.
The sacrifice moved my spirit and gave me a great healing.

To the folks keep trying me
    Playing with my name
  Imma tell you this straight up
   This shit is not a game
Don't take my smile for weakness
  Or the way I talk as a joke
   That's how you end up missing
Cops will be looking for prints in a scope
On your mom's porch they'll find a note
  A cut out tongue that was once yours
   I'll be nice enough to have it in a gift tie
In a lake tied to bricks yo pussy ass shall lie

                -Mayer

Get a stupid prize

To the folks keep trying me.
Playing with my name.
I'm gonna tell you this straight up.
This shit is not a game.
Don't take my smile for weakness.
Or the way I talk as a joke.
That's how you end up missing.
Cops will be looking for prints in a scope.
On your mom's porch they'll find a note.
A cut out tongue that was once yours. There will be a
surprise at each door.
I'll be nice enough to have a gift tied.
In a lake tide to bricks you're gossiping as will lye.

Baby I know I'm stressing you out

I'm in this bitch I'm not talking bout no girl

Youre a rider and that's no doubt

You shine like the moon but youre my world

You hold me high like a pillar

You hold me down like gravity

I can't wait to hold my wife

In-2-U-I-C .... Intimacy

You... I think about daily

You... I dream of every night

Us.. We are forever

Forever.... and the after life

Mateo

that missed feeling

Baby I know I'm stressing you out.
I'm going crazy thinking about my girl.
You're a rider and that's no doubt.
You shine like the moon but you're my world.
You hold me high like a pillar.
You hold me down like gravity.
I can't wait to kiss and hold my wife.
In-2-u-i-c…… intimacy.
You… I think about daily.
You…. I dream of many nights.
Us…. We are forever.
Forever… and the after life.

Have you ever wondered does God hear a thug cry?
Even tho I've committed many sins.
People like me was born to lose
And we had to build ourselves to win
My dreams are now nightmares
Lord do you hear my cries?
Will I wake up the next day?
Or will my spirit rise?
Please deliver me from my enemies hand.
God I'm no longer an evil doer.
God I know I'm not the perfect man
For now I watch how I manuever
My heart is heavy like the sand of the sea
I wish to be pure like the honey from a bee
I feel trapped like a nat in a spider web
Hoping you hear my cry to free and save me
I want to be close to you like a moth loves light
Please accept me for who I am today
I know I wasn't living right
So I just pray, pray, pray, pray and pray.....

- Maiyui

Asking for acceptance

Have you ever wondered does God have a thug cry?
Even though I've committed many sins.
People like me was born to lose.
We had to build ourselves to win.
My dreams are now nightmares.
Lord do you hear my cries?
Will I wake up the next day?
Or will my spirit rise?
Please deliver me from my enemies hand.
God I'm no longer an evil door.
God I know I'm not the perfect man.
For now I watch how I maneuver.
My heart is heavy like the sand of the sea.
I wish to be pure like the honey from a bee.
I feel trapped like a net in a spider web.
Hoping you hear my cry to free and save me.
I want to be close to you like a moth loves light.
Please accept me for who I am today.
I know I wasn't living right.
For I just pray, pray, pray, pray, and pray.

Hey mama I'm sorry I've put you through this pain.
I never meant to cause you this hurt
The thought of what you're dealing with is insane.
I know this hurt more than when you gave birth.
Mama you used to carry me in your whomb
Now you're here carrying me through this
I can't wait to get out and hug you tight
And feel genuine love thru your kiss
Please mama no more tears
Unless they're tears of joy
Our Family has been thru so much in these years
The new life we will enjoy....
Each other's company with all your kids
Your grandkids and our spouse
We no longer will run the streets
Because Allah will continue to bless our house
Mama every time we talk
You tell me God has a plan
Mama I know I was once your baby boy
But now you must look at me as a man.

- Mayor

Mom dukes

Hey Mama I'm sorry;
That I put you through this pain.
I never meant to cause you this hurt.
the thoughts of what you're dealing with is insane.
I know this hurts more than when you Gave birth.
Mama you used to carry me in your home.
now you're here carrying me through this.
I can't wait to get out and hug you tight
and feel genuine love through your kiss.
Please Mama no more tears.
Unless they're tears of joy.
Our family has been through so much in these years.
The new life we will enjoy…
Each of theirs company with all your kids.
Your grandkids and our spouse.
We no longer will run these streets.
Because Allah will continue to bless our house.
Mama every time we talk.
You tell me God has a plan.
Mama I know I was once your baby boy
. But now you must look at me as a man.

I used to kick it with them in the old days
   They never asked if I was okay
   Alot of folks stayed in my face
   As long as I had my money
   I used to be on the backstreet
   Now I'm stuck in Rice Street
     This is the concrete jungle
       Full of hungry beast!
   Allah has shown me I'm heading to the top
         Yall I promise I won't stop
         One time I busted down a brick
           Like a karate chop
         OG tells me to keep it cool
This experience has me want to go to law school
     Never show what you're working wit
       That's how you become a lick.

            - Mayes

Back street

I used to kick it with them in the old days. They never asked
if I was okay.
A lot of folks stayed in my face.
As long as I had money.
I used to be on the back street.
Now I'm stuck in rice street.
This is the concrete jungle.
Full of hungry beast!
Allah has shown me I'm heading to the top.
Y'all I promise I won't stop.
One time I busted down a brick.
Like a karate chop.
O.G. tells me to keep it cool.
This experience has me want to go to law school.
Never show what you're working with.
That's how you become a walking lick.

Be impeccable w/ your words
You must speak things into existence
Never go against the grain
Because you could be finished for resistance
Learn not to gossip
Or talk behind anothers back
Jealousy is a hating trait
And I'll never get that
The mind is a powerful thing
Think and it shall be true
Actions have consequences
So be careful of what you do
To creticize is to judge
To critique is to help
One is bad for the soul
The other is good for your health
The tongue isn't a heavy muscle
Yet many hasn't mastered the strength to hold it
Quit thinking you're being attacked
Just listen and be silent
If you TRULY want to better yourself
You must understand your flaws
In order to open your mind for change
You must allow your pride to fall...

YOU HAVE TO CLAIM IT

BE IMPECCABLE WITH YOUR WORDS.
YOU MUST SPEAK THINGS INTO EXISTENCE.
NEVER GO AGAINST THE GRAIN.
BECAUSE YOU COULD BE PUNISHED FOR
RESISTANCE.
LEARN NOT TO GOSSIP.
NOR TALK BEHIND ANOTHER'S BACK.
JEALOUSY IS A HATING TRAIT.
AND I'LL NEVER GET THAT.
THE MIND IS A POWERFUL THING PERIOD THINK
AND IT SHALL BE TRUE. ACTIONS HAVE
CONSEQUENCES.
SO BE CAREFUL OF WHAT YOU DO.
TO CRITICIZE IS TO JUDGE.
TO CRITIQUE IS TO HELP.
ONE IS BAD FOR THE SOUL.
THE OTHER IS GOOD FOR YOUR HEALTH.
THE TONGUE ISN'T A HEAVY MUSCLE.
YET MANY HASN'T MASTERED THE STRENGTH TO
HOLD IT.
QUIT THINKING YOU'RE BEING ATTACKED.
JUST LISTEN AND BE SILENT.
IF YOU TRULY WANT TO BETTER YOURSELF.
YOU MUST UNDERSTAND YOUR FLAWS.
IN ORDER TO OPEN YOUR MIND FOR CHANGE.
YOU MUST ALLOW YOUR PRIDE TO FALL…

★ I refuse to be a supposed to be, who's a wanna be,
that's pretending to be happy... that aint me!

★ I refuse to be what people want me to be? not living
to be who I know I can be,? then I look in the mirror
not recognizing who I see.

★ If you only knew what I've overcame in my life ? on
the streets... A hater would be like oh okay... but a
supporter would be proud of me.

★ I'm proud of myself ? love what I've become... I remind
myself daily this is the beginning ? I'm far from done.

★ I'm titled many things but I'm far from a failure... If I
failed anything it's your expectation to be the perfect person...
Something that doesn't exist.

★ No matter how much money you have, how many friends you got,
nor how many trophies you collected ... you need to hear this!

★ With the snap of a finger ? the blink of an eye that shit
can disappear... memories will fill your void, confussion will replace
love, ? many thoughts will appear.

★ Material things can be stripped away ? anything with feet can
walk away... Even your own shadow is there when it's sunny
days but during dark times it cast away....

★ To be in the world with billions of people whos energy
can be transfered through a handshake or a smile... Remember
rivers that flow supplies resources but when used too
much they can be dried like the Nile!!!

Mayer

IR2

64

I REFUSE TO BE A SUPPOSED TO BE, WHO'S A
WANNA BE COME THAT'S PRETENDING TO BE
HAPPY… THAT AIN'T ME!
I REFUSE TO BE WHAT PEOPLE WANT ME TO BE
AND NOT LIVING TO BE WHO I KNOW I CAN BE
AND THEN I LOOK IN THE MIRROR NOT
RECOGNIZING WHO I SEE.
IF YOU ONLY KNEW WHAT I'VE OVERCAME IN MY
LIFE AND ON THE STREETS… A HATER WOULD BE
LIKE OH OK… BUT A SUPPORTER WOULD BE
PROUD OF ME.
I'M PROUD OF MYSELF AND LOVE WHAT I'VE
BECOME… I REMIND MYSELF OF DAILY THIS IS THE
BEGINNING AND I'M FAR FROM DONE.
I'M TITLED MANY THINGS BUT I'M FAR FROM A
FAILURE… IF I FAILED ANYTHING IT'S YOUR
EXPECTATION TO BE THE PERFECT PERSON…
SOMETHING THAT DOESN'T EXIST.
NO MATTER HOW MUCH MONEY YOU HAVE, HOW
MANY FRIENDS YOU GOT, NOR HOW MANY
TROPHIES YOU COLLECTED… YOU NEED TO HEAR
THIS!
WITH THE SNAP OF A FINGER AND THE BLINK OF
AN EYE THAT SHIT CAN DISAPPEAR….
MEMORIES WILL FILL YOUR VOID, CONFUSION
WILL REPLACE LOVE, AND MANY THOUGHTS WILL
APPEAR.
MATERIAL THINGS CAN BE STRIPPED AWAY AND
ANYTHING WITH FEET CAN WALK AWAY… EVEN
YOUR OWN SHADOW IS THERE WHEN IT'S SUNNY
DAYS BUT DURING DARK TIMES IT CAST AWAY…
TO BE IN THE WORLD WITH BILLIONS OF PEOPLE

WHOSE ENERGY CAN BE TRANSFERRED THROUGH A HANDSHAKE OR A SMILE… REMEMBER RIVERS THAT FLOW SUPPLIES RESOURCES BUT WHEN USED TOO MUCH THEY CAN BE DRIED LIKE THE NILE!

Faith without work is dead and hope without belief is a lie.

Faith is keeping a smile on your face even when you want to cry.

Faith is not letting go because something inside is holding on

Faith is knowing your time is coming even tho it may seem long

Faith is believing God's plan. Faith is staying strong.

Faith is knowing you're a peasant who will one day take
the throne.

Some of the strongest people give up when things aren't
going our way.

Faith is trusting that God hears our cries so don't keep
asking for the same thing when you pray.

Faith reminded me to worry about the things I can control.

Many great things shall happen once we decide to play
our roll.

- Maya -

FAITH

FAITH WITHOUT WORK IS DEAD AND HOPE
WITHOUT BELIEF IS A LIE.
FAITH IS KEEPING A SMILE ON YOUR FACE EVEN
WHEN YOU WANT TO CRY.
FAITH IS NOT LETTING GO BECAUSE SOMETHING
INSIDE IS HOLDING ON.
FAITH IS KNOWING YOUR TIME IS COMING EVEN
THOUGH IT MAY SEEM LONG.
FAITH IS BELIEVING GOD'S PLAN. FAITH IS
STAYING STRONG.
FAITH IS KNOWING YOU'RE A PEASANT WHO WILL
ONE DAY TAKE THE THRONE.
SOME OF THE STRONGEST PEOPLE GIVE UP WHEN
THINGS AREN'T GOING OUR WAY.
FAITH IS TRUSTING THAT GOD HEARS OUR CRIES
SO DON'T KEEP ASKING FOR THE SAME THING
WHEN YOU PRAY.
FAITH REMINDED ME TO WORRY ABOUT THE
THINGS I CAN CONTROL.
MANY GREAT THINGS SHALL HAPPEN ONCE WE
DECIDE TO PLAY OUR ROLE.

I once told you that I had a dream that you relapsed

You promised me you'd stay strong; that the devil can't trick you.

I listened to your words and ignored my gut feeling.

By now you should know that we are spiritually connected and
I feel the things you do.

Trust me I feel your hurt of us not seeing each other so I call
everyday to ease your pain.

Knowing that you're out there doing what you're doing; How do you
expect me to stay sane?

Put down the bottle; pick up a bible; put down the drugs they're
not good for your soul.

Please get back to the strong, beautiful, and loving woman I know
you are and allow God to take control.

Behind these walls all I do is think of you. At times I blame
myself for what you're going through.

We are blessed and almost done so why give up when were almost through?

Please do this for me, your other kids, but most of all yourself. You are my
heart, my soul and I will ALWAYS love you in this life, after death!
♡ Dad and [illegible]   Mack 8/4/22 3:37am

TAKE BACK YOUR LIFE

I ONCE TOLD YOU THAT I HAD A DREAM THAT YOU
RELAPSED.
YOU PROMISED ME YOU'D STAY STRONG AND
THAT THE DEVIL CAN'T TRICK YOU.
I LISTENED TO YOUR WORDS AND IGNORED MY
GUTS FEELING.
BY NOW YOU SHOULD KNOW THAT WE ARE
SPIRITUALLY CONNECTED AND I FEEL THE THINGS
YOU DO.
TRUST ME I FEEL YOUR HEARTS OF US NOT SEEING
EACH OTHER SO I CALLED EVERY DAY TO EASE
YOUR PAIN.
KNOWING THAT YOU'RE OUT THERE DOING
WHAT YOU'RE DOING; HOW DO YOU EXPECT ME
TO STAY SANE?
PUT DOWN THE BOTTLE AND PICK UP A QURAN OR
BIBLE, PUT DOWN THE DRUGS THEY'RE NOT GOOD
FOR YOUR SOUL.
PLEASE GET BACK TO THE STRONG, BEAUTIFUL,
AND THE LOVING WOMAN I KNOW YOU ARE AND
ALLOW GOD TO TAKE CONTROL.
BEHIND THESE FOUR WALLS ALL I DO IS THINK OF
YOU.
AT TIMES I BLAME MYSELF FOR WHAT YOU'RE
GOING THROUGH.
WE ARE BLESSED AND ALMOST DONE SO WHY GIVE
UP WHEN WE'RE ALMOST THROUGH?
PLEASE DO THIS FOR ME, YOUR OTHER KIDS, BUT
MOST OF ALL YOURSELF.
YOU ARE MY HEART AND MY SOUL AND I WILL
ALWAYS LOVE YOU IN THIS LIFE AND AFTER

DEATH!

Today shit was unreal. I woke up from a good dream to a
nightmare.

People I would lay down my life for turned against me; something
I wouldn't dare.

I've been passed judge for no reason, no reason at all.

It's up to me to stand & lean on my own not to fall.

I can't grasp my thoughts about how something like this
can go on.

So I must focus on the task at hand, keep faith, and
stay strong.

Only Allah and myself knows what my future has
instore

For I am a man on the outside. For I am a man in the
CORE..!

SWITCHED SIDES

TODAY SHIT WAS UNREAL.
I WOKE UP FROM A GOOD DREAM TO A
NIGHTMARE.
PEOPLE WHO I WOULD LAY DOWN MY LIFE FOR
TURN AGAINST ME; SOMETHING I WOULDN'T
DARE.
I'VE BEEN HAS JUDGE FOR NO REASON, NO
REASON AT ALL.
IT'S UP TO ME TO STAND AND LEAN ON MY OWN
NOT TO FALL.
I CAN'T GRASP MY THOUGHTS ABOUT HOW
SOMETHING LIKE THIS CAN GO ON.
SO I MUST FOCUS ON THE TASK AT HAND, KEEP
FAITH, AND STAY STRONG.
ONLY ALLAH AND MYSELF KNOWS WHAT MY
FUTURE HAS IN STORE.
FOR I AM A MAN ON THE OUTSIDE.
FOR I AM A MAN TO THE CORE!

Real pain is being betrayed when you're in your lowest
phase.

Hurt by those who you thought loved you and now
you're in a misguided place.

My kindness is selfishness, my love is hate, and my
spirit has been consumed.

My smile has evaporated and I feel like a heavy
burden, I'm talking tidal waves and a full moon.

Cheerful is what I was. I was willing to give everything.

Misery loves company so I engaged her with a wedding
ring.

Useless and used, tortured and bruised, misunderstood and
unloved, and now I'm confused.

Unwanted and taunted.... Mentally distraught....

To sum up my feelings... I'm currently lost!!!

LOST PAIN

REAL PAIN IS BEING BETRAYED WHEN YOU'RE IN
YOUR LOWEST PHASE.
HURT BY THOSE WHO YOU THOUGHT LOVED YOU
AND NOW YOU'RE IN A MISGUIDED PLACE.
MY KINDNESS AND SELFISHNESS, MY LOVE IS HATE,
AND MY SPIRIT HAS BEEN CONSUMED.
MY SMILE HAS EVAPORATED AND I FEEL LIKE A
HEAVY BURDEN; I'M TALKING TIDAL WAVES IN A
FULL MOON.
CHEERFUL IS WHAT I WAS. I WAS WILLING TO GIVE
EVERYTHING.
MISERY LOVES COMPANY SO I ENGAGED HER WITH
A WEDDING RING.
USELESS AND USED.
TORTURED AND BRUISED.
MISUNDERSTOOD AND UNLOVED.
NOW I'M CONFUSED.
UNWANTED AND TAUNTED…
MENTALLY DISTRAUGHT…
TO SOME OF MY FEELINGS…
I'M CURRENTLY LOST!!!

How can I stay calm with all this shit going on in my
life?

My mom is busting her ass at that job makes me
want to cry.

My father and little sister hurting so they're getting
drunk off gin.

My lil brother is growing to be a better man.

My big sister is striving for a greater change.

Me.... well.... I'm striving to stay sane.....

Fuck a friend and these folks who ain't shit.

Fuck the grimey females who was on their knees
sucking my dick.

Fuck the people who had ~~my bottle and got~~ got ghost.

I'm repeling anything thats negative. I refuse to
let that shit to get close.

Mayor

AT THE END OF THE DAY

HOW CAN I STAY CALM WITH ALL OF THIS SHIT
GOING ON IN MY LIFE?
MY MOM IS BUSTING HER ASS AT THAT JOB MAKES
ME WANT TO CRY.
MY FATHER AND LITTLE SISTER HURTING SO
THEY'RE GETTING DRUNK OFF GIN.
MY LITTLE BROTHER IS GROWING UP AND TRYING
NOT TO SIN.
MY BIG SISTER IS STRIVING FOR A GREATER
CHANGE.
ME… WELL… I'M STRIVING TO STAY SANE…
FORGET A FRIEND AND THESE FOLKS WHO AIN'T
SHIT.
FORGET THE GRIMY FEMALES WHO WAS ON THEIR
KNEES SUCKING MY STICK.
FORGET THE PEOPLE WHO HAD GOT GHOST.
I'M REPELLING ANYTHING THAT'S NEGATIVE.
I REFUSE TO LET THAT SHIT GET CLOSE.

Part of being humble is being humiliated;
Especially when you're destined to be great.

I thank Allah for bettering me;
I would've been gotten a hater ate for a deputy plate.

Folks
~~make~~ make assumptions after they hear your charge;
They swear they're the judge, jury, & prosecutor.

They take shots behind your back and on the court,
And try to label themselves a shooter.

Now they're acting like plumbers by bringing up old shit;
Real eyes realize real lies that's why they gets no wit.

Behind these walls people can be whoever they pretend to be;
I stay to myself and believe 1% of what I hear & 99 of what I see.

In the streets many have no motion;
They probably never been outside 285.

Many were imprisoned in the mind before they got here;
They're just living but never experienced being alive!

— Mayor

WORRY BOUT SELF

PART OF BEING HUMBLE IS BEING HUMILIATED;
ESPECIALLY WHEN YOU'RE DESTINED TO BE
GREAT.
I THANK ALLAH FOR BETTERING ME; I WOULD
HAVE BEEN GOTTEN A HATER HATE FOR A
DEPUTY PLATE.
FOLKS MAKE ASSUMPTIONS AFTER THEY HEAR
YOUR CHARGE; THEY SWEAR THEY'RE THE JUDGE,
JURY, AND PROSECUTOR.
THEY TAKE SHOTS BEHIND YOUR BACK AND ON
THE COURT; AND TRY TO LABEL THEMSELVES A
SHOOTER.
NOW THEY'RE ACTING LIKE PLUMBERS BY
BRINGING UP OLD SHIT; REAL EYES REALIZE REAL
LIES THAT'S WHY THEY GET NO KICK IT.
BEHIND THESE WALLS PEOPLE CAN BE WHOEVER
THEY PRETEND TO BE; I STAY TO MYSELF AND
BELIEVE 1% OF WHAT I HEAR AND 99 OF WHAT I
SEE.
IN THE STREETS MANY HAVE NO MOTION; THEY
PROBABLY NEVER BEEN OUTSIDE 285.
MANY WERE IMPRISONED IN THE MIND BEFORE
THEY GOT HERE.
THEY'RE JUST LIVING BUT NEVER EXPERIENCED
BEING ALIVE!

You _never_ want to listen.
You _always_ want to be heard.
You'll stay quiet for a second
But you can't repeat a phrase or a word.
    Many times I bit my tounge;
    To keep our bond intact.
But for now on I want communicate;
Because it takes 2 people to do that.
    I talk; you ignore
You scream instead of talking.
    You move off emotions.
    That's why I'm walking.
    Away from it all....
    Away from this life.
I'll struggle on my own.
Because love has no price.

                    - Mayor

CLOSED EARS

YOU NEVER WANT TO LISTEN.
YOU ALWAYS WANT TO BE HEARD.
YOU'LL STAY QUIET FOR A SECOND; BUT YOU
CAN'T REPEAT A PHRASE OR A WORD.
MANY TIMES I BIT MY TONGUE.
TO KEEP OUR BOND INTACT.
FOR NOW ON I WANT TO COMMUNICATE. BECAUSE
IT TAKES TWO PEOPLE TO DO THAT.
I TALK; YOU IGNORE.
YOU SCREAM INSTEAD OF TALKING.
YOU MOVE OFF EMOTIONS.
THAT'S WHY I'M WALKING…
AWAY FROM IT ALL.
AWAY FROM THIS LIFE.
I'LL STRUGGLE ON MY OWN.
BECAUSE LOVE HAS NO PRICE.

Currently I'm hurting wishing I was home.

Feeling trapped and helpless. I feel so alone.

Knowing that I'm loved hurts right now.

I can't believe it.

It hurts that I'm loved but can't recieve it.

This isn't a place for any human. This isn't civilization.

It takes a different type of person to stay here. It feels like a mental stabilization.

— Mayor

CURRENTLY

CURRENTLY I'M HURTING WISHING I WAS HOME.
I'M FEELING TRAPPED AND HELPLESS.
I FEEL SO ALONE.
KNOWING THAT I'M LOVE HURTS RIGHT NOW.
I CAN'T BELIEVE IT.
IT HURTS THAT I'M LOVED BUT CAN'T RECEIVE IT.
THIS ISN'T A PLACE FOR ANY HUMAN…
THIS ISN'T CIVILIZATION.
IT TAKES A DIFFERENT TYPE OF PERSON TO STAY HERE…
IT FEELS LIKE A MENTAL STABILIZATION.

Cry, young man cry.
It's okay to cry.
Hurt young gent hurt.
You're human & this is Earth.
Fight young warrior fight.
You can make it through the night.
Rise young king rise.
Know your time will come.
You've bared so much pain.
Now the pleasure has just begun.

- Mayor

BOYS CRY

CRY YOUNG MAN… CRY.
IT'S OK TO CRY.
HURT YOUNG GENT… HURT.
YOU'RE HUMAN AND THIS IS EARTH.
FIGHT YOUNG WARRIOR FIGHT YOU CAN MAKE IT
THROUGH THE NIGHT.
RISE YOU KING… RISE.
KNOW YOUR TIME WILL COME.
YOU'VE BARED SO MUCH PAIN.
NOW THE PLEASURE HAS JUST BEGUN.

It's said that family is all you have and I don't doubt
that, but how do you define family?

Is it: Blood, goals to become more, or can it be simple
loyalty?

Every family has different characteristics, the funny
one, the athlete, the one with all the brains.

Every family is different and one can't be compared to
being the same.

Some families cherish holidays and some enjoy vacations

Mom and pops become overjoyed when they find out
they're grandparents in the making.

Sunday dinners and family cookouts are ways to unite
and bond.

Family are those who makes you happy and on rainy
days they bring out the sun

Mayor

FAM TIGHT

ITS SAID THAT FAMILY IS ALL YOU HAVE AND I
DON'T DOUBT THAT, BUT HOW DO YOU DEFINE
FAMILY?
IS IT: BLOOD, GOALS TO BECOME MORE, OR COULD
A SIMPLE BE AS SIMPLE AS LOYALTY?
EVERY FAMILY HAS DIFFERENT CHARACTERISTICS:
THE FUNNY ONE, THE ATHLETE, THE ONE WITH
ALL THE BRAINS.
EVERY FAMILY IS DIFFERENT AND ONE CAN'T BE
COMPARED TO BEING THE SAME.
SOME FAMILIES CHERISH HOLIDAYS AND SOME
ENJOY VACATIONS.
MOM AND POPS BECOME OVERJOYED WHEN THEY
FIND OUT THEY'RE GRANDPARENTS IN THE
MAKING.
SUNDAY DINNERS AND FAMILY COOKOUTS ARE
WAYS TO UNITE AND BOND.
FAMILY ARE THOSE WHO MAKE YOU HAPPY AND
ON A RAINY DAY THEY BRING OUT THE SUN.

Today is one of those days that I'm really feeling this pain.

Trapped, bored, & locked away. this shit has me going insane.

Broken phones & broken TV's like we're niggas with broken mindsets.

We're fed sloppy food & drank tap water like were unloved pets.

Phone calls makes time go by but sometimes it hurts to hear folks living without you

I'm planning for a second chance of life because I know what Imma do

The places Imma go & the things Imma indulge in

The people Imma avoid & the events Imma attend.

The women & food Imma smash.

The checks Imma cash...

DON'T WORRY ABOUT TODAY

TODAY IS ONE OF THOSE DAYS THAT I'M FEELING
THIS PAIN.
TRAPPED, BORED, AND LOCKED AWAY… THIS
SHIFT HAS ME GOING INSANE.
BROKEN PHONES AND BROKEN TV'S LIKE WE'RE
MEN WITH BROKEN MINDSETS.
WE'RE FED SLOPPY FOOD AND DRINK TAP WATER
LIKE WE'RE UNLOVED PETS.
PHONE CALLS MAKES TIME GO BY BUT SOMETIMES
IT HURTS TO HEAR FOLKS LIVING WITHOUT YOU.
I'M PLANNING FOR A SECOND CHANCE OF LIFE
BECAUSE I KNOW WHAT I'M GOING TO DO.
THE PLACES I'M GONNA GO AND THE THINGS I'M
GONNA INDULGE IN.
THE PEOPLE IMMA AVOID AND THE EVENTS I'M
GONNA ATTEND.
THE WOMEN AND FOOD IMMA SMASH.
THE CHECKS IMMA CASH…

I know you may ask me what the fuck I did to get myself in this situation.

Shid... I'm just like you. curious and clueless.

Out of all of my dreams and accomplishments being incarcerated wasn't on my to do list.

Was it too much pride by feeling untouchable?

Maybe it was being to humble by being so accessible.

— Mayor

THE PEOPLE WANT TO KNOW

I KNOW YOU MAY ASK ME WHAT THE HELL I DID
TO GET MYSELF IN THIS SITUATION.
HID… I'M JUST LIKE YOU… CURIOUS AND
CLUELESS.
OUT OF ALL MY DREAMS AND ACCOMPLISHMENTS
BEING INCARCERATED WASN'T ON MY TO DO LIST.
WAS IT TOO MUCH PRIDE BY FEELING
UNTOUCHABLE?
MAYBE IT WAS BEING TOO HUMBLE BY BEING SO
ACCESSIBLE.

This story is about changes because many of us are afraid of change.

It contains a caterpillar, shellfish, and human; 3 different species but one of the same.

FEAR is abbreviated for False Evidence Appearing Real; the thought alone can cause pain.

1st I'll tell you about a caterpillar that moved slow like a person who owes you money but took off like a fast moving jet plane.

Afraid to go through metamorphis it was scared to go into its cacoon but in reality it was truly afraid to be by itself.

Thinking that it would be missing out on everything not knowing being out the way was avoiding problems which was good for its health.

It went into its cacoon, gave his body some rest, and got its mind right.

A few weeks later it came out one of the most beautiful & strongest butterflies that ever took flight.

The shellfish was used to its shell, it's body grew, and it's shell stayed it's regular size.

The shellfish saw others change their shell as they grew but it didn't want to accept change and that became its demise.

The shellfish got so comfortable and grew bigger in its shell.

It grew so big that it couldn't move and it suffocated itself.

The human was an observer and saw things for what they are.

The human said they could get comfortable like shellfish or be like the caterpillar and go far.

Change isn't as bad as we make it seem we must get uncomfortable and away from what were used to.

Sam Cooke quoted a change is gonna come but my question is when it comes.. what will you do?

Choice to change

This story is about changes because many of us are afraid of change.
It contains a caterpillar, shellfish, and human.
Three different species but one of the same.
FEAR is abbreviated for False Evidence Appearing Real; the thoughts alone can cause pain.
First I'll tell you about a caterpillar that moved slow like a person who owes you money but took off like a fast moving jet plane.
Afraid to go through metamorphosis it was scared to go into its cocoon but in reality it was truly afraid to be by itself.
Thinking that it would be missing out on everything not knowing being out the way was avoiding problems which was good for its health.
It went into its cocoon and gave its body some rest, and got its mind right.
A few weeks later it came out one of the most beautiful and strongest butterflies that ever took flight.
The shellfish was used to its shell as it's body grew; its shell stayed its regular size.
These shellfish saw others change their shells as they grew but it didn't want to accept change and that became its demise.
The shellfish got so comfortable and grew bigger in its shell.
It grew so big that it couldn't move and it suffocated itself.
The human was an observer and saw things for what they are.
The human said they could either get comfortable like the shellfish or be like the caterpillar and go far.
Change isn't as bad as we make it seem we must get uncomfortable and away from what we're used to.
Sam Cooke quoted a change is gonna come but my question is when it comes… What will you do?

I was encouraged to keep writing no matter how painful or hard.

Truth is I'm hurting so deep inside and I'm falling apart.

My voice was once powerful; It was heard like a lion's roar.

Now when I attempt to talk to someone I'm shunned and ignored.

Family is always distracted and the lawyer is always busy with another case.

Friends are living their best life... So I'm stuck looking for a place...

A place where I belong... A place to call home...

A place where I feel safe... Somewhere not alone...

Two dollars and fifty cents an hour; I'm litterally paying for folks time.

Lord knows I ask for forgiveness for some of the thoughts that has crossed my mind....

Losing it slowly

I was encouraged to keep writing no matter how painful or
hard.
Truth is I'm hurting so deep inside and I'm falling apart.
My voice was once powerful; it was heard like a lion's roar.
Now when I attempt to talk to someone I am shunned and
ignored.
Family is always distracted and the lawyer is always busy with
another case.
Friends are living their best life… so I'm stuck looking for a
place…
A place where I belong…
A place to call home…
A place where I feel safe…
Somewhere not alone…
$2.50 an hour; I'm literally paying for folks time.
Lord knows I ask for forgiveness for some of the thoughts
that has crossed my mind…

Time... So deadly but so kind.

Time can heal deep wounds but it can also kill the mind.

The waiting game is something that comes with growth.

It can be simple like opening a present or as
anxious as a couple awaiting birth.

As the seconds hand tic fast and the minutes too
behind.

Hours slowly pass and days intertwine.

Months are now years.

Filled with lessons, tears, trials, and cheers.

Something that seems so far away can be very close and
near.

Time can seem to be staying still for someone who is
impatient.

But once the blessing reveals itself you'll see why
Allah had you waiting.

— Maya

Worth the wait

Time that that that so badly but so kind.
Time can heal deep wounds but it can also kill the mind.
The waiting game is something that comes with growth.
it can be simple like opening a present or as anxious as a
couple awaiting birth.
As the seconds hand tick fast and the minutes toc behind.
Hours slowly passed and days intertwined.
Months are now years.
filled with lessons, tears, trials, and cheers.
Something that seems so far away can be very close and
near.
Time can seem to be staying still for someone who is
impatient.
But once the blessing reveals itself you'll see why Allah had
you waiting.

Jointed, out

They say we jointed out but truth be told we
in the joint

In the day room backs stay on the wall & you
must sleep with a knife to stay on point

One light fixture can make a shank, wick or a fire
to cook a sausage

We cut it up, but the soaps down, & use the shower
water to make a packet

In the streets some of us wore designer &
some people wore whatever

Now we're tailoring our red jumpsuits to fit, making
pants out of sweaters.

We used to smoke out of backwoods but now it's
bible paper & brown napkins mixed with cocoa.

We used to run from ~~the police~~ 50 now our runs getting
to make money
made by the C.O.

Fine, ugly, big bone, or nocas we get happy when we see
a female in the hall.

Aint no call outs just rec call since we only get flip flops
we doing barefoot playing basketball.

To add flavor to their bologna sandwhiches some
people put powdered Koolaid on the meat.

Drug abusers buy strips instead of hygiene, when
they're released they'll have missing teeth & fucked up feet.

Sinners come in and pretend to be big believers of
God.

Folks ~~who~~ who was hard that had a gang in the streets
become the quitest ones in the pod.

we use
The same sink ~~to~~ brush our teeth ~~we use~~ wash out
trays, and our clothes.

Shit gets so real some people wash their clothes in
the toilet bowl.

Many people would say these things are pointed out
but to me I say we improvise.

Weve learned to adapt to the hard situations and
use both our mind & ~~talent~~ to survive.

        — Mayor   6/29/22

Jointed out

They say we jointed out but truth be told we in the joint.
In the day room back stay on the wall and you must sleep
with a knife to stay on point.
One light fixture can make a shank, wick, or a fire to cook a
sausage.
We cut it up, but the soups down, and use the shower water
to make a pocket.
In the streets some of us wore designer and some people
wore whatever.
Now we're tailoring our red jumpsuits to fit and making
pants out of sweaters.
We used to smoke out of backwoods now it's Bible paper
and brown napkins mixed with cocoa.
When making money we used to run from the 5.0 now to
make money our runs getting made by the C.O.
Fine, ugly, big bone, or no ass….. we get happy when we see
a female in the hall.
No call outs just rec call.
Since we only get flip flops we go barefoot playing basketball.
To add flavor to their bologna sandwiches some people put
powder kool-aid on the meat.
Drug abuses by strips instead of hygiene, when they're
released there have missing teeth and messed up feet.

Sinners come in and pretend to be big believers of God.
Folks who was hard that had a gang in the streets become the
quietest ones in the pod.
We use the same sink to brush our teeth, wash out trays, and

our clothes.
Things get so real some people washed their clothes in the
toilet bowl.
Many people would say these things are jointed out but to me
I say we improvise.
We've learned to adapt to the hard situations and use both
our mind and family to survive.

A YEAR LATER

I was asked how come I no longer excercise nor write

Is it possible for a broken wing bird to take flight?

Can a vehicle with no gas arrive to it's destination?

Is a bear lazy because it slept longer during hibernation?

My experiences are one of a kind...

The stories are unbelievable!

I have blank paper and full pens, so how come writing
feels unachievable?

I have sneakers to run, So why is it hard to take
the first step?

Only those who truly loves you hears when you are upset

So is losing the motivation to write and the gain of
weight me calling out for help!

— Mayer

A year plus change

I was asked how come I no longer exercise nor write.
Is it possible for a broken wing bird to take flight?
Can a vehicle with no gas arrive to its destination?
Is a bear lazy because it slept longer during hibernation?
My experiences are one-of-a-kind.
The stories are unbelievable.
I have blank paper and full pens.
So how come writing feels unachievable?
I have sneakers to run.
So why is it hard to take the first step?
Only those who truly love you hears when you are quiet.
So is losing the motivation to write and the gain of weight me
calling out for help?

Why? Why am I going through this?

I went from a scholar, motivational speaker, administrator, coach, business owner to become an inmate in prison.

Usually I'm shown the upmost respect in my Cole Haan's & tailored suit

Despite what they see I'm more than an inmate in cheap sandals, uniformed in white & blues.

I've saved lives in the streets.

I enlighten minds with my speech.
I create change with my actions.
I display unconditional love with my passion.
But where am I now?
Sleeping on a metal bunk. No longer in my Cali King sized bed.
No longer enjoying homemade meals. Waiting to hear the words "chow call" to be fed.
No longer booking flights for confernces or vacations w/ family and friends.
Here I'm staring out the window in my cell wishing to be free like the wind.
Why? Why am I here?
Convicted of a crime I did not do.
I was taken from my family by a system I once pledged my allegiance to.
An alleger who's known for lying, an allegation, and no proof.
I will continue to fight for my freedom & tell my story that's the truth.
Why? Why me?
I've come to learn from the stories I've been told.
It's possible Allah can be using me, the way he used Yusuf & Job.
Job lost everything and received more in abundance.
Yusuf was imprisoned for a crime he didn't commit.
Turned out their circumstances was a blessing not a punishment.
The first four letters in message is mess. There was a message in the mess.
Allah is using my story to change the system. I am truly blessed. No more whys...

No more whys

Why? Why am I going through this?
I went from a dude in the hood, to a motivational speaker,
administrator, coach, business owner, to becoming an inmate in prison.
Usually I'm shown the up most respect in my Cole Haans and tailored
suits.
Despite what they see I'm more than an inmate and cheap sandals;
Uniform and white and Blues.
I've saved lives in the streets.
I enlighten minds with my speech.
I create change with my actions.
I display unconditional love with my passion.
But where am I now?
Sleeping on a metal bunk no longer in my Cali king size bed.
No longer enjoy homemade meals.
Waiting to hear the words "chow call" to be fed.
No longer booking business flights or vacations with families and
friends.
Here I'm staring out the window of my cell wishing to be free like the
wind.
Convicted of a crime I did not do.
I was taken from my family by a system I once pledged my allegiance
to.
An alleger who's known for lying, an allegation, and no proof.
I will continue to fight for my freedom and tell my story that's the
truth.
I've come to learn from the stories I've been told.
It's possible Allah can be using me the way he used Yusuf and Job.
Job lost everything and received more in abundance.
Yusuf was imprisoned for a crime he didn't commit.
Turned out their circumstances was a blessing not a punishment.
The first four letters in message is mess.
There was a message in the mess.
Allah is using my story to change the system.
I am truly blessed.
No more whys…

Mom dukes and I during a visit.

To whomever comes into contact with this book I pray that you received a little motivation from it. It's important as humans that we learn: religion, constitutional rights, financial literacy, morals, etiquette, trades, how to defend ourselves, and one of the most important lessons we should be taught is unconditional love.

To any incarcerated individual that is locked up. I pray your bid is smooth. Guilty or innocent it's important to take the time to develop yourself and continue to enhance your mind, body and soul. So when you do get home you'll be a better person than you was coming in.

To the innocent inmates serving time...... DO NOT QUIT FIGHTING! It's a hard battle. It's possible to win. It's worth the fight!

To my community thank you. You all NEVER gave up on me and I'm appreciative for the love, trust, and support.

To my friends thank you all for helping me stay mentally sane.

To my family I love you all and I'm extremely proud of the strength you all have shown.

To whomever is feeling down... always remember rather you know it or not.... There's someone who loves you.

"This is only one of many more books to come."
-Mayor Sanchez Yusuf waller

ABOUT THE AUTHOR

Born and raised in Atlanta, Georgia. Mayor Sanchez Yusuf

Waller is an activist who dedicated his entire career and lifestyle to helping better the lives of others. At the peak of his career he was falsely accused of a crime he did not commit. Uneducated of the legal and "justice system" he decided not to focus on the legal battle he was unknowingly fighting. Sanchez assumed that the truth was common sense and expected the accusation to be revealed as a lie. Well common sense is not common.

Convicted and punished for a crime he did not commit. Sanchez is working backwards with his legal team, family and community to prove his innocence and be vindicated.

Mayor Sanchez Yusuf Waller is using his experience to prevent others from falling into the legal traps set by wolves. Waller is attempting to enlighten people of the crooked games the injustice system plays.